DEAR READER,

I'm so grateful that you're picking up this book. Its message has been sparking in my heart for some time now. When I originally had the idea, I balked. But God made it clear that it wasn't about my ability - He simply asked "Do you want to be a part, Em?"

So friend, these pages are my match - I've struck it into a flame, and I'm throwing it down in faith that something catches fire in your heart today too.

For too long, a large part of the Christian community has been mauling the interpretation of I Timothy 2:12. Disregarding context, culture, and even the example Jesus Christ Himself gave, to ostracize an entire sex from preaching the gospel freely.

I wrote this book with three clear intentions:

1) To honor the women heroes of Bible times. There are beautiful parts of God's heart that are uncovered in their stories, even if sometimes their stories are hard to tell.

2) To encourage women of all ages to step fully into their true identity as an equal child of God, and not let anything stand in the way of God's calling on their life.

3) To rebuke common lies and misinterpretations about a woman's equal part in the Christian community and the Kingdom of God.

I intentionally chose rhymes to tell these stories, because I want even the littlest women to be encouraged, inspired, and understand how important their voice is to the Kingdom of God.

Jesus had a radical view on equality. He was known for bucking cultural norms and was recorded again and again valuing and championing women as equal parts of God's heart.

I have two little women myself, and can't have them growing up thinking their sex is a disability when it comes to building His kingdom. And you know what? I can't have you believing that either.

So I implore you Girl, Preach - Share the love of His word!
There's a big world that needs your voice to be heard.

Much love,

DEDICATED TO MY HEROES,

Esther, Iris, Brenda, Crystal,
Amy, Rachel & Hannah

A GIRL PREACH! initiative

www.girlpreach.com

Copyright © 2022 by Emily van den Heever
All rights reserved. This book or any portion thereof may not be reproduced or used in any manner whatsoever without the express written permission of the publisher except for the use of brief quotations in a book review.

OF WOMEN BIBLE HEROES

(& some other truths too)

EM VDH

Anna was a prophetess, she told of things to come. People listened to her, because she listened to God, hope and truth were her anthem.

B

Bathsheba survived some unjust stuff, but she didn't let that define her! She rose above it, became a powerful queen, and shared her wisdom with others.

C

Chloe was a leader in the early church, her household lived in the light.

She knew being a leader meant to keep learning, asking questions is always alright!

D

Deborah was a prophetess and judge, a decision maker in old Israel.

She courageously marched with Israel's armies, and foretold how their enemies would fall.

E

Eve was the very first woman, God made her purposely different than man.

Women and men are equal parts of God's heart, both made in His image and plan.

F is for femininity, it's a pretty long word, but it's half of God's heart planted special in every woman, created to be seen and heard.

G is for God-Given,
equal dominion over the earth.
He gave Eve and Adam
equal responsibility,
and also equal worth.

H

is for Helper, the description God tasked Eve, but this word in hebrew means "rescuer", one who looks out for those in need.

Iscah is a bit of a mystery, but her name means 'to see'. She most likely saw visions of what could be in the future, that's called the gift of prophecy.

Jael was a quick thinking creative, she didn't hesitate when there were hard things to do. She picked up her tools and got to work, she rescued the whole of Israel too!

K is for King Jesus!
Our redeemer and our friend.
He highly valued women, even when others didn't, and brought God given equality again.

M

Mary Magdalene was the first to see Jesus, after he rose again! His visit to her first was on purpose, she was His follower, but also His friend.

Noa was one of five sisters that demanded an unfair law change. God agreed with them, and their equal rights as women, and a new, just law was made.

Priscilla was a missionary! She planted churches too. She shared God's love wherever she went, and owned her own business too!

Q

Queen Esther was an Israelite, she was beautiful and brave. She spoke up for those who couldn't, and God gave her a nation to save.

R

Rahab loved adventure, she hid spies and helped God's people. She knew how to make deals and communicate clearly, and she's a great grandma in Jesus's family!

S

Shiphrah was a midwife in Egypt of old, she was ordered to do wrong, but didn't do what was told.

She stood up for what she knew was right, and God blessed her courage as she lived in the light.

T

Tamar was hurt physically by someone close, but even in the dark, she kept her voice, and wisdom too, she wasn't afraid to speak up.

U

Understand when Jesus won over sin and death, He fixed the fall of man. Women should not be seen as less than, or held under any dominion.

W

The woman at the well is a very special story, Jesus breaks down social boundaries as He shares His love and glory.

Because no matter where someone has been or where they are from, Jesus's love and freedom is for everyone.

E-X-traordinary! Is Mary, Jesus's mom, she said a big 'yes' to God. She wasn't afraid even though she was young, she knew He would not lead her wrong.

This Y is special because the hero is **you**. You are God's daughter, and He has given you a special thing to do.

He's tasked us, women and men alike, to share the hope of His love, to be the light.

Z zz

So don't fall asleep,
don't go silent or retreat.

GO - HERO GIRL,
SHARE THE LOVE OF GOD'S WORD.
THERE'S A BIG WORLD THAT
NEEDS YOUR VOICE TO BE HEARD!

www.ingramcontent.com/pod-product-compliance
Lightning Source LLC
LaVergne TN
LVHW070435080526
838201LV00133B/283